Birth
Certificate

ALSO BY JOHN VALENTINE

*Beginning Aesthetics:
An Introduction to the Philosophy of Art*

Close to the Fallen

The Heart of the Matter

Birth Certificate

Selected Poems

JOHN VALENTINE

BIRTH CERTIFICATE

Copyright © 2025 by John Valentine

All rights reserved

An Imprint of Monte Ceceri Publishers

Cover photograph © 2025 by Ed Eckstrand

Epigraph from the poem "Water Wheel" by Linda Pastan, *PM/AM: New and Selected Poems* (New York: W. W. Norton & Company, 1982).

No part of this book may be reproduced, stored in a retrieval system, or transmitted by any means, electronic, mechanical, photocopying, recording, or otherwise, without written permission from the publisher or author, except in the case of brief quotations embodied in critical articles or reviews.

For additional information, press inquiries, bulk or educational purchases, and other resources, please contact Monte Ceceri Publishers.

Valentine, John, 1948– author
Birth certificate / John Valentine
ISBN: 978-1-949512-22-9 (paperback)
ISBN: 978-1-949512-23-6 (eBook)
1. Poetry. 2. Philosophy — Buddhist philosophy. 3. Philosophy, Modern — Existentialism. 4. Philosophy — Idealism. 5. War — Moral and ethical aspects. 6. Religion and culture. I. Title

Monte Ceceri Publishers
Savannah, GA
www.swanhorse.com
www.montececeri.com

You want a life
as simple as a cup
of rain.

— *Linda Pastan*

Acknowledgments

Amethyst Review: "Bashō and Wallace Stevens"

Big Table Publishing:
"Belief" • "The Day the Meteor Comes" •
"Doubt" • "To Nashville with George Jones" •
"Seventeen" • "What's Ahead of You"

Confluence: "Vultures"

The Midwest Quarterly: "Feng Shui"

Mudlark: An Electronic Journal of Poetry & Poetics:
"Abraham and Isaac" • "Gettysburg" •
"Unknown Soldier" • "Wild Words"

Muscadine Lines: A Southern Journal: "Writing"

The Penwood Review: "Prophets"

Pif Magazine: "Riddle of the Clover"

Pudding House Publications:
"Avant-garde" • "Baby Needs New Shoes" • "Birth Certificate" •
"Breaking Through to the Dolphins" • "Buchenwald" •
"Duplicity" • "The Empiricists of Savannah" • "Eucharist" •
"Homeless" • "Infatuation" • "Jugglers" • "Koan" • "The Last
Days of Buffalo Bill Cody" • "*Lavender Mist*" • "Lilacs" • "The
Man in the Car" • "Moonshine" • "My Father's German" • "One
Thing at a Time" • "Postscript to Castro" • "The Sensualist" •
"Shooting Pool with Buddha" • "Sitting Bull" • "Strip Club" •
"Summer" • "Things" • "Villa" • "The War Between Duty and
Desire" • "What's Behind You" • "Wild Geese"

Scarlet Leaf Review: "Sandhill Cranes"

Southern Poetry Review: "Voodoo"

Contents

Acknowledgments vii

Birth Certificate 15
Infatuation 16
Seventeen 17
Strip Club 18
Eucharist 19
My Father's German 20
On My Last Night as a Child, His Sleep Was Final 21
Feng Shui 22
Back 24
What's Ahead of You 25
House of the Poets 26
Jugglers 27
The Wanderer 28
The Empiricists of Savannah 30
Duplicity 31
Vultures 33
The Culling 34
Rose Hill Cemetery 35
Unknown Soldier 36
The Faces: In Memoriam 37
Koan 40
Bashō and Wallace Stevens 42
Shooting Pool with Buddha 44

The Sensualist   45
Homeless   47
Because the Night   48
Wild Geese   50
Postcard from 1945   51
Doubt   52
Things   54
Voodoo   55
Sandhill Cranes, Savannah   56
Polemic Against Roses   57
Riddle of the Clover   58
The Day the Meteor Comes   59
Big   60
Dinner with Emily Dickinson   61
Barbecuing with the old Chinese Masters   62
My Hero   63
Belief   64
The War Between Duty and Desire   65
Moonshine   66
Lavender Mist   67
The Egyptian   68
Laying on Hands, North Georgia   69
Prophets   70
Abraham and Isaac   71
Barking While Music Stirs Among the Grasses and Leaves   72
One Thing at a Time   73

Breaking Through to the Dolphins   74

Landscape of the Saxophone   75

To Nashville with George Jones   76

The Man in the Car   77

Baby Needs New Shoes   78

Lilacs   79

Gettysburg   80

Clotilda   81

The Last Days of Buffalo Bill Cody   82

Sitting Bull   83

Villa   84

Postscript to Castro   85

Water   86

Prisoner   87

Krishna at the Potter's Wheel   88

International Day of the Disappeared   89

Avant-garde   90

Summer   91

The Body's Hope   92

What's Behind You   93

Wild Words   94

Alchemy   95

Writing   96

About the Poet   99

Birth Certificate

Birth Certificate

Nothing like launching a new ship
with a paper bottle of champagne.

Interesting facts, you suppose.
Length, weight, a little splash,

displacement in the sea of beings.
Sometimes a whole handprint,

like the record of a headstand
or somersault in the thin air of

existence. And then, as if it only
happens once, you only get one,

filed away for the mandarins. But
listen, listen to the water lapping

at your bow, see how the sun's
always like a new woman walking

on the waves. And every night, in a
different port of call, you're signing your

certificate with the moon upon your shoulders,
the sea tumbling in your ears,

and your heart throbbing like a child,
born again and trembling,

all wet and flushed and ready for the dawn.

Infatuation

Let's just say you're sixteen
and Nietzsche is the wild wolf

ghosting the moon.
What use would you have

for saints, the tuxedo
of etiquette?

Wouldn't you run away
with the wind?

Strange how a well speaks loudest
when no one dips into its secrets.

Even the weakest vines
find a place in the light.

What will grow will grow.
And if you speak of sparking,

remember the surging stars,
the radiant sun,

the gypsy dawn crossing its legs
and laughing,

leaning back like a boy
in the green hammock of the trees.

Seventeen

Many summers later I'd learn to love
the shadows illumination creates.

— *Stephen Dunn*

Yin was once the dark side
of a mountain, yang
the scatter of sun
in every flower.
Dualism, clarity
a matter of choosing sides.
Elemental
to have an enemy
who was always wrong,
an audience
you never really saw.
All the while
missing everything,
inconclusions of the heart,
twilight's
simple complexity,
the truth
of sand shifting its feet,
the tide running away,
like conviction,
pulling everything out to sea.

Strip Club

Expecting something more than flesh,
imagine

the young boy's naïveté: why stop
with the skin?

It's not the truth he'd come for.
He wanted

singularity, the bare particular.
There's something

calm and clean, he thought, about
taking everything

off and standing naked in the light.
Just the soul,

pulsing in its neon. Just the many nights
he watched

the sky strip the moon of clouds, waiting
on its beauty.

Just the glow, shining at the core. Just
the roses

pinking now in the cigarettes and smoke.

Eucharist

— For J.H.

Sundays, those deep days of rest along the banks of the St. John's,
wading among the quiet creatures who also worshipped the glory
of the sun: tadpoles skittering in the sheen, possums ambling, a high
hawk lifting in the clouds. Two poles waited and we were fishers
of the dawn. Like an acolyte, I helped you with the host, the soft body
we laid upon the water. In the blood of the rising sun, I learned to look
deeper than the surface. I learned to fathom beauty, mark the stirrings
of the spirit. You taught me how to wait and keep silent. Everything
was holy, everything shimmered in the bright cathedral of the pines.
What grace there was in your cast. How the line snapped and settled.
How patient were your hands. Cicadas droned, dogwoods spread their
blaze. I learned to see the frog kneeling in the lilies, the magic play
of colors, the slow step of the heron. I learned too, when the brilliant
bass was writhing in my hand, how to bow, how to worship, how to
give back just as much as I'd been given.

My Father's German

Little Sprachspiele,
language games bright as a ribbon.
Children's rhymes, sing-
song. The words smooth
as anisette, the taste
of early years.
Until the stroke
that took away your house,
left a few stones standing,
odd and unconnected,
non sequiturs, bits of rubble,
the scatter in your eyes.
Silence, days when the wind
came and nothing stirred,
stillness in the air.
And then, all at once,
in full timbre, over
and over, the music,
bright and clear, the sweet
and sudden German.

On My Last Night as a Child, His Sleep Was Final

—*After Larry Levis*

The blur between twilight and night. Hard to say exactly

where the line is, like a man losing his hair. Which final one

is it? Which one and then we say *bald*? Which sleep and the boy says *grown*?

On my last night as a child, he didn't die. He left, shadows closing

around him, like darkness. Someone stayed behind, though. He seemed

faraway, nothing more to say. We all knew. But it wasn't the sudden stroke,

not lightning that opened my years. Isn't the past something

that pushes us? Eliding, something gained, something lost. In time

I wasn't much wiser, nor taller. Maybe something newer, like looking back

at a chrysalis, an old suit that no longer fit, his empty shoes, something sensed,

lifting into light.

Feng Shui

—*For My Father*

Cathedral oaks are best.
The wind prefers rough surfaces,

the informality of wood.
The rain speaks softly

in the secret words of water.
The moon hangs

like a lantern in the night.
Halfway down a hill

with the priesthood of worms
he's rooted in the earth.

The air is like a memory,
compelling in its fragrance and must.

He lies with the moss,
settles in the weeds,

the wet leaf graves.
Chiaroscuro, the right place,

a balance of darkness and light.
The day draws him

through subtle sluices
of the dead.

He stirs, rises with the beetle,
the grub that works its way

toward wings,
the maggot that blossoms

like a sudden flower
only with the surest compass,

unerringly,
always at the heart of everything.

Back

It's not as if you could keep
a good man down forever.

What's a little mortality among
friends. Gone and buried, or

maybe a reliquary, ashes kept
in a cigar box over the mantle.

Anticipations. You said you'd be
back. That old oak in the

yard, the way it crooks in the
limbs, that sway. The scatter

of birdsong, insouciant, high
in your leaves. That old bark,

tough enough, but really generous,
protective, like a good slicker

in the rain. And who's to say
the wind in your width is not a

whisper? Even now the children gather
under your branches. Even now you tell

a story of roots, dependability. If we
sit with you often, if we linger, it's

just something familiar, a memory,
something swaying in the years.

What's Ahead of You

Epidermal disappointments, to be sure,
as the gravity of your fall
begins its diaspora of the mirror,
picaresque in the wanderings of the flesh.
Think of it as papier-mâché, an impression
increasingly too large and too soft
for your deeds.
Follicular disenfranchisement,
no more seeds on the windswept crown of the king.
Only a single hair bridging the Continental Divide.
Thermodynamics, the clockmaker
forgetting to wind his clock.
Everything flying away from everything,
memories from accomplishments,
love from the closest caress,
like a comet on its fiery way to forever,
as the black hole at the horizon
of your hands
turns time to the stillness of stone.
What comes once will never come again,
though the heart runs like a roan stallion
in the greener pastures of its dreams,
your eyes are hopelessly young,
and desire, ah desire, how it lifts
like a radiant egret in the spreading shimmer
of the moon.

House of the Poets

moths, ladybugs, even the wind
stirring the leaves says to trust
instinct's music

—*Khadijah Queen*

It will, of course, sit by the sea. Shutters
thrown

open to the whirl of wind, the scent of
summer air.

A thousand moons, no two ever the same.
An ark

of animals and friends whose names
are wild

and whispered. A Tower of Babel. No
tongue turned

away. The spell of words. A large porch
for pilgrims

in the midst of splendor. Every door ajar,
windows wide,

the house swaying, saying yes and yes,
again and again.

Come in dear friends, come in.

Jugglers

The poet is a light and winged and holy thing.
— *Plato*

Their wild words haunt like ghosts
in a soaring swirl

of swish and swing that rises and
reels

in the thin air of their entrechats. How
the quick verbs

rocket into rhythm, orbiting them like
a sun.

How the flaming lines spin and light the air.
What a web

they weave where nothing ever falls, not even
death.

All is lean and lithe, everything a feather.
Not even night

can stop them now, not even gathering dark,
as high above our heads

they throw their words and watch them spin
and sail,

suddenly soaring, flying surely to the stars.

The Wanderer

I stop somewhere waiting for you.
— *Walt Whitman*

Look for me in the weeds as they drink
the blessing of the rain,

how their feet are like hands holding on,
their hats like

all the colors of the sky. Beyond desire
they climb the air,

its staircase, the surging ladder of the sun.
I will be the tramp

with soft eyes, the wanderer on the far side
of forever.

Linger a while. Hear the leaves and the wind
whisper words,

feel the rhythm of their rhyme. Every breath
waiting quietly,

hoping to be heard. You will find me again
by the wounded,

sitting up all night with the dying, teaching
them how to let go,

coming and going, the lesson of life everlasting,
the pulse of the House of Being.

Nothing ever ends. Look closer, see the generations
of the soul. Even when we part I'll be with

you. And you with me. The poem will never end.
Come, sit by my side.

We will live it again and again.

The Empiricists of Savannah

Strict constructionists, they have not
come for abstraction,
but for flesh, the senses,
the way the world rubs against them
with all its sudden urgency.
Injudicious azaleas, explosive dogwoods,
sweet honeysuckle wrapping itself
around the wind.
The quick chorus of bees,
everything buzzing in the sun.
Seeing is believing, they exclaim,
at the temple of colors,
as they cross the old town
like a carnival
with all the exuberance of a blind
man who stumbles on a cure
for winter and night
in the swirling rods and cones of spring.

Duplicity

Bless duplicity in all things.
— *Rodney Jones*

Bless the worm of the false at the heart of the true.
What glorious skin,

what fabulous fiction, grows from such a seed.
Panoply of masks

and colors. Drama of dissimulation. All honor
to the black widow,

its hourglass of time. The cactus flower, the
sanguine eye

of the hurricane. What delicious dances of deception.
Bless the wisdom

of veils, makeup, the craftiness of words. Hosannas
for summer in

Antarctica. For dead stars whose light has come so far,
like voices

from beyond the grave. For atoms and quarks, those
porous centers

of substance. Can we know the sun but for shadows?
The moon but for

its other side? Purity and its partner do their duel,
their *pas de deux*.

O universe, o hustler of being, bless the impossible
sheen, the bubble

of life. And always, always, bless the worm of the false
at the heart of the true.

Vultures

You've seen the last lovers of the dead,
the casual loop, the long drift of their
desire. Who can glimpse them without
shuddering? They flock to the fallen
deer and the rigid mud turtle with a
hunger fierce as fire. The dust roils,
they rise like banshees in the fury
of their quick concern. They scatter
bones to the wind, take a torn heart
and give it wings. They lift like angels
in the bright halo of the sun. You flush
the fields in silence, leaning closely
in the hunt. And there, deep in the dawn,
where the sky hurries hunters to blood,
you see with the wild eye of your eyes,
hear with the raw ear of your ears,
touch with the red hand of your hands.

The Culling

— For James Dickey

It was time. Shredded greens, squash
like rotting crescent moons. Gardens

swept by a scythe. All night, deer
at the windows. Early, he gathered

himself. The rifle, the box of Remingtons.
Staring down something somewhere

beyond the idea of it. Leaving. But
needful, necessary. High then in

winter woods. Tracks, a steel stand, claws
gripping, like the cold. Sighted, the big

buck nosing the air, steaming. A clean
shot. Impossible to miss. But taking it,

taking it... Startled, every nerve on fire,
recoiling, he brought him down. The snow

deepened. Darkness. The long path home.
Wind shifting. He knew his bed would

open. He knew his wife would stir, murmur,
put her hand upon a stranger.

Rose Hill Cemetery

—*Macon, Georgia*

The narrow lanes and sharp angles weren't made for modern convenience.

This is sacred ground that has to be walked, and we rounded the terraces, like those

of purgatory. Matthew, a bad storm, had left its mark. Scattered limbs, debris,

but mostly a giant oak uprooted, the Bobcat crew working overtime to save the

Confederate graves where they were sliding down to the Ocmulgee River

and oblivion. But these were men not meant for water, the foreman's eyes

seemed to say. Something remembered, sacred. And the crew came together

in the late autumn light. Just like both sides after the Civil War they were trying

to put together broken lives and stones, something worth saving, that for a while

was ripped apart in the chaos of a thundering storm.

Unknown Soldier

—*Laurel Grove Cemetery, Savannah*

Can yearning rise in moonlight?
He might have left long ago,
his spirit
rifling straight as a bullet to home.
Soft grass.
The distant farm, unknown
then too.
He might have left only in the wind,
without a whisper.
But this boy. *This* one. Right here.
His broken
bones. *He* never left. Even without
a name
he never left. Can ground be
erasure?
Can it hide him, like a lost memory,
always in the roots, always
on the far side
of forever?
Can it only do what dirt does?
Can it only forget?
In this garden of the dead, no sound
awakens him.

The Faces: In Memoriam

1. Auschwitz

The condition of everything tends toward the condition of silence.
— *Charles Wright*

Everything collapsed. Gold fillings,
piles of glasses, shoes.

Camp whistles screaming, infallible,
always on time.

The sound of string quartets. Mozart
at the gate. Men here, women

and children there. Showers. All night
the sound of trains. Inexorable

clocks. Relentless, indifferent. Liberators
with horror caught in their throats, like falling

into hell. Days when the bones rattled. Days
of blood and ash. Days when the wind

stopped and nothing, nothing could be heard
but silence.

2. Buchenwald

Broken armature
scattered in the yards,
bones settled in a heap.
Piles of shoes, ragged coats,
glasses that read the fine print
of the sun.
Bone collectors
did the work of the rats.
Sirens.
Here, the Sabbath was a working day.

***

Sotto voce:

The rabbis put G-d on trial.
Everything unraveled,
went right to the bone.
Just flesh, running and raw,
like cattle late for a train.
The wind rose,
swept through the sheaves like a scythe.
There was no question of innocence anymore.

***

Shabbat:

A candle,
some spittle of water for wine.
In the back rooms
after the guards' beatings,
the light flickered,
the rabbis stuttered in the dark.
Acquittal.
High in the clouds,
a prayer, the scatter of stars,
the bloodred skin of the moon.

Koan

A man gives away all his worldly possessions
and enters a Zen monastery. The sensei is old
and kindly and gives him his own koan:

how many hands does the wind have?
Ah, thinks the man, this will be easy. He lays
out his tatami mat and begins to meditate long

and hard, filled with the expectation of success.
Day after day he sits, losing himself deeper
and deeper in thought. Images come by the

thousands, swirling like bats in the vast wind
organ of the night. Diaspora of seeds. Maybe,
he says to himself, the old man wants me to think

of the air, how a hawk wears the wind like a skin.
Or maybe it's the utter buoyancy of a leaf,
the lean of a ship on the waves. Or even

a feather he once saw fluttering in the dawn.
On and on he rambles. Everything comes, nothing
comes. How hard is the discipline of words.

The years pass. The sensei's eyes are pools of
compassion. His fellow monks are quiet and
respectful as the strange man sits and thinks.

Everyone feels his desire, everyone wishes
him well. The snow settles and soon he's
nothing but a memory, the silence of stone,

as the wind, which had never, never left his side,
rises like a lover and wraps its arms, its infinite hands,
round the shoulders of his grave.

Bashō and Wallace Stevens

What I love about language is what I love about fog:
What comes between us and things grants them
their shine.

— *Mark Doty*

How many times can a koan stub the mind's toe?
Or a sensei clap his one hand

with the suddenness of sound? Here it is, late at night,
and you've come together,

two old friends who never knew each other. Stillness,
whispering leaves,

and a promise that only things themselves can make,
or the moon as the ghost

of everything possible. Step in, step in, and together
we'll go down the long

darkened hallway in the House of Being, down to the last
window at the end

where the stars glimmer in the flickering light, like a scatter
of coins.

And later, when fog becomes a thief clouding the moon,
what better veil

than the mist? I've fallen in love with illusion. And if I whisper,
tell you the truth of my life,

that I lean on your lines, will you come and sit by my side
while I read,

read everything into your words?

Shooting Pool with Buddha

Live your life as if you were already dead.
—*Zen saying*

As inscrutable as a three-rail kiss,
his smile is quintessential
detachment, the way a blonde
in stiletto heels and infallible
cue can take your heart away
while waiting, she says,
near a street corner
for the Out-of-Town Express.
Booze and bright lights
and compassion.
The Eightfold Path of Perfection.
But nothing is like the stillness,
the quiet code of his hand and eye,
enlightenment in a free man's aim,
the rising rhythm of his stroke,
while the moon is a backlit bulb,
and the balls are clicking
like crickets
in the empty pockets of the air.

The Sensualist

You want a life
as simple as a cup
of rain.

—*Linda Pastan*

The otherworldly intentions of others
having become all too apparent,
the sensualist took refuge in the world
of the senses, the prospect of pleasure
his only solace in times of the rapture
and other sorts of mass departures. His
refusal to accept another world was like
a bee whose lack of speculation is a way
of visiting every stamen of spring. But
spirit isn't soul, he said, nothing separable
from the dèlicatesse of his fingers and tongue,
or the quick code of the world tapping his eyes
and his ears. Everything sparked on his flesh.
He found joy in Nietzsche, the idea that everything
would return with no illusion of memory,
again and again, like an endlessly forgotten
elegy. He wrote volumes about lilies, their
infinite fragility. He praised the virtues of dung,
the beauty of contrasts, and worshipped the dawn
in the bright sanctuary of the sun. He stared for
hours at ants. Everything glistened. And finally,
in a gesture of love, he painted the world in forms
so exact that no one could see the strokes or the

subtle difference, only a certain sheen that shone
through the shadows, like the ambient light
of a full moon. Wordless then, he waited and
saw that all he wanted from the air was a whisper,
a passing cloud, a rainbow, in a life as simple
as a cup of rain.

Homeless

What's madness but nobility of soul
At odds with circumstance?

— *Theodore Roethke*

At home once in the universe,
the old physicist

used to weave theories of everything
in the cat's cradle

of his mind. How orderly the atoms
danced,

how fleeting the half-life of years.
Wrapped in rags,

his words are spoken now to the wind.
He signs the language

of loss, hands tangled in mudras,
like a manic Buddhist,

or an operator at the switchboard of
chaos,

pulling wires, answering calls, frantically
making connections

on the dizzying streets of delirium.

Because the Night

—*For Patti Smith*

Far from shore on the waves of a dream
is that you

I see, like a lighthouse, your beam so
steady,

its long arm of truth, rising from pain
and the dark?

Love will always reach out, no matter
the storm.

If I call it redemption, if I say I see
the terrible times,

everything overcome, the flashing in
your eyes

on the far side of despair, if I say all this
it's an elegy,

an admission of love. I never could live
without you.

Never. No matter now if we're closer
to the end,

no matter if the coldest night is all
there is,

I'll hold your hand and see the light,
because the dark

cannot have us yet, because the night
was made for lovers,

and so were we.

Wild Geese

The old holy men of India stood in the raw sun
for years in refusal

and clenched their fists until nails grew through
the backs of their hands,

like lilies. Why is the world so hard? Wet roses
nodding in the rain

show you their beauty. Soft willows fall to their knees,
you'll gather all the

spirit you need. What more can you ask of wild geese
who wear the wind

like a shadow? What more can they give you? At last
nothing's left but light,

luminous and pure. You linger, breathe the stillness,
wait for nothing now

but the moon and an endless arbor of stars.

Postcard from 1945

— For My Mother

You sent it to your own mother long ago.
Bathing Beach, La Jolla.

How it traveled from California to Boston
to Savannah

to land in these old hands, I cannot say.
I like the front

of it, more like a painting than a photo.
Is that you

in the sombrero sun hat? Everything almost
posed,

stylized, like something by Renoir. A good day.
You even

said so: *What a beautiful day I've had. I never
have seen*

such beauty. You left for good a while back, but
keeping this card close

is like holding your hand. I can almost feel
the sand and the sea

that day as if we were swimming side by side,
shining, like nothing,

nothing would ever darken the days ahead.

Doubt

One size doesn't fit all. Imagine the big one,
Descartes in his nightclothes,

doubting everything: his body, the world, even
doubt itself, though the latter

brought him to the one sure nub of things where
he quickly asked God to bring

it all back again. Nothing like an empty world
on the way to certitude.

But consider the cousins, the smaller members
of the family. Ever doubt your best friend?

Or maybe that moment before a speech as if
the restless audience

really were paying attention? Or the sudden
uncertainty before your first kiss?

Isn't it like a quick catch in your throat, the heart
running like a roan stallion

in a forest of footfalls? Doubt is the great goad,
the stimulus, the eerie stranger

who taps you on your shoulder at a dance
and quickens your pace

as you glide across the floor with all the thrill
and anxiety

of someone who knows their very next step
could be the bravest

or last they will ever try to take.

Things

So much eros in a normal room!
— *Stephen Dunn*

What sheer intimacy in the easy chair,
its leathery touch returning
like an old memory. And why not caress
that sofa, long-serving and comfortable

as a lover. See how it wants to put its arms
around you. The rug has lain down
its life, sacrificing at the feet of desire.
If you turn to the windows, it's only

because everything's clearer that way.
Vistas for the drifting days. Even
the crocus in its Oriental pose seems to
lean, wanting to be closer. The porcelain

cat curls its tail and purrs. That moon-eyed
wind chime blows you a song. Things
tremble with a secret life. And then in
the evening the whole room rises with desire,

hurries, follows you up the stairs. Speak
softly now as you would to a lover. Hold it
closely. There, in the dark, take its hand.
Whisper love's nothings, again and again.

Voodoo

Chicken claw and bat wing,
eye of newt. Hair sprig and
toenail shards. That doe-eyed
doll in the hangman's noose
is you. Blood feud, the half-life
of hate is forever. You get the point,
over and over. Nothing now
but rosaries and exorcism,
mumbled incantations. Every
mirror's cracked. The mail's
stopped, the dog has left for
good. Santa Maria! Somewhere
on the far side of forgiveness, she's
up tonight, caftaned and calculating,
cold as a bayou priestess, putting
pins in the memory of love.

Sandhill Cranes, Savannah

Tidal pools. Migrating visitors
in the relentless kiln.

This quiet pond, though, an oasis
of relief. Its peaceful

shade contagious and cool as
wings are spread

in silence. Semaphores: a fan dance
or maybe mating.

No matter. Dignity and grace
understood, shared.

We watched for a week how they
preened, how they lifted

and landed without a ripple. Noiseless.
What is the world

if not a stopping point, a moment
in passing? One day,

deep in the shadows of the wind,
they were gone.

Polemic Against Roses

Dreadful hothouse stems nestled in
sweat. Pure black blossoms from hell.

Or dead ones pressed ingloriously
in a book. Long-limbed crimson

carnage: the boutonnière, bouquet,
last kiss of the casket. Such shows

are easy, insincere. We shall not praise
them for effortless effort. Misplace

our love. But rather circumspection,
consideration of luminous light, the peonies,

phlox, brown-eyed Susans by the road.
Lilies of the field. After midnight

by the milk of an ivory moon, they will
rise, lift their arms, dance in secret

places no long-stemmed legs can go.

Riddle of the Clover

Perhaps it's like the Sphinx's riddle. Some of us when born

arrive with four leaves. What do we know about luck, we who shiver

in the rain like children? We only see you down on your knees among us.

Is it worship or greed? We're crushed. Some of our weathered friends

live with two leaves, like umbrellas in the sun. Merciless, there's never

enough shade. But our elders, the survivors, sign the trinity, ancient wisdom

you never acknowledge. You ignore us underfoot. We're tired of callous shoes.

We raise our green hands in the prayer of all anchorites: pass us by in peace.

The Day the Meteor Comes

Let's just hope it's not a big one,
like the one that hit Jupiter
a while back,
took out a chunk nearly the size
of Earth.
But you can't be subjunctive all
the time.
Think of it as a marathon and you're
the runner.
Stops, starts, sometimes a little
walking, sometimes you take a cab
to get a leg up on the others.
No one holds survival against you.
Who has time for affairs of the sky?
But take care.
Remember the tricks the sun can play,
like the time you gave up
on a high fly ball, lost it in the glare,
and fifteen minutes later, like Lazarus,
you had the luxury of coming to,
remembering nothing.
Those are the days you wonder about,
a little unsettled, checking
your blind spot, watching for sudden shadows,
and recollecting as best you can
the latest odds of a fastball blazing right
down the middle of the solar system,
high and hard, a strike
on the inside corner of your life.

Big

The Jains believe the soul of an ant
is as large
as that of an elephant. Such reverence
is as generous as the peacock tail
swish
that delicately ushers to one side
or another
the smallest beings scuttling on the byways
of our lives.
But the mystery perhaps is not generosity
but astigmatism.
Beyond the savanna, swirls of endless
galaxies, everything
moving away
from everything else, strings stretched
to infinity
and beyond.
The largest number, the last universe,
impossible.
And the souls of ants in the Mirrors
of Being are the faces
of Krishna
reflected forever. We once
were this big.
We still are. And will be
again and again.

Dinner with Emily Dickinson

Perhaps you'd prefer a sonnet, she said,
something metaphysical

in its délicatesse, its couplets deliciously
predictable.

The main course could feature an elegy,
not unlike

a paean to Achilles in his days of mourning
Patroclus,

accompanied by a bright bouquet, a love poem
to sweeten the palate.

And then, in the study, an after-dinner aperitif,
an ode to liberty

from the Romantics. No thanks, I said. Something
brief and lean,

if you please, like a haiku, something deeply wrought
and piercing,

as if on the tip of a pen, written by a recluse and sequestered
for many years

until at last the right guest came along and heard the voice
sounding beautifully

from the very back of the room, hidden in a closed drawer.

Barbecuing with the old Chinese Masters

Sunday afternoon in the backyard
and the Dao's in perfect harmony.

Confucius says: The gentleman knows
gentility and the limits of beer.

Moderation. Stillness in the autumn
air, wisdom in the gathering friends.

Ting is the ultimate carver. Nineteen years
and his blade has yet to hit the bone.

Lao-tzu, in his barbecue apron, does nothing
more than nothing, cooking by not cooking.

The rotisserie turns itself, round and round
in glory. Chuang-tzu eases in a lounge chair,

dreaming of a butterfly dreaming of him.
Mencius bows to the food, thanking

the fields, the farmers, civilization. Yan Hui,
greatest of students, serves everyone ahead

of himself. Old Peng blesses the blossoms
of the garden. And the quiet calm of Li Po,

isn't it like a conductor's baton finding the right
key, the tempo, the oneness of everything

in the sweet tinkling of the dinner bell, echoing
over and over in the fading light.

My Hero

There's much to be said for Aristotle's
dry microscope

and Plato's hot-air balloon ride
to the heavens.

Both were sometimes late to dinner.
Hats off to Nietzsche,

steel-eyed and wandering in the Alps.
And to Hume, that lover

of billiards and doubt. Kudos
to skeptics, rationalists,

and of course nihilists, those bad boys
who believe in nothing at all

except nothing. Praise be to them all.
But my hero is Bashō, who spoke to the

frogs, who smiled and put beauty
on the head of a pin

where no one suspected, so sharply
not even a dragonfly could possibly stand it.

Belief

Isn't it like the tourist who fails to produce
a passport at the border

and cannot cross into the sure land of certainty?
Poseur, a person with no support,

no gravitas, who rushes to the edge of the world
with every expectation,

seeing everything everywhere, the many faces
of figures in a puzzle

that aren't there. Shadows, a shift in the wind,
nothing more.

The epistemologist's towheaded stepchild.
But oh how often belief

oversteps the darkness, and the stars seem crystalline,
more mysterious for the leap,

somehow nearer, while knowledge curls up in the
House of the Known

with its tired facts whose best days are behind them,
like old memories

just within the reach of yesterday's grasp.

The War Between Duty and Desire

Skirmishes deeper than
skin-deep,
dendrites lighting up like
a small city of electric lights,
peptides sparking,
cells swept away by
sudden tsunamis,
wave after wave of
frenzied flooding.
The heart races nearby,
like a bloodred stallion,
hands are nervously wringing,
and somewhere at the back
of the brain
the old moralist piles sandbags
again and again
at the bamboo doors —
lost in the carnage,
he knows:
millions will die,
no prisoners will be taken.

Moonshine

No anisette, no sweet elixir
of the gods. Nothing less
than liquid lightning, flash

and fury, the way it thunders
through the brain like a rumbling
summer storm. Keeper of the fog,

radiator diesel, the one true
democrat. You blur family
and work and dry seasons

of the years. You make misery dance,
light and ecstatic. Suffering sings
like a hound. O brotherhood of man!

O snake charmer and carpetbagger.
You take away our debts like any
charlatan, and give us smoke, sleight

of hand, and amnesia, but only for a while,
then pack up, grin, and disappear,
returning everything with double interest due.

Lavender Mist

— For Jackson Pollock

Sometimes the cat rolled
in the bright galaxies,
smearing constellations,
like a comet on its fiery way
to forever. The old shaman
with his bottle of beer
just laughed and put on
the blues.
Cat claw, fur balls, chaos.
Such the making of a world.
Was there meaning in the mist?
It means everything or nothing.
Paint is the only god.
And what temples there were
where the priest would dance
for days. The night was a tangle
of stars, and everything swirled
but the cat who licked his paws
and yawned, and slept for years
in the maelstrom.

The Egyptian

He certainly didn't look like one,
young and tuxedoed
and lost. A black and white
beauty, feral and free,
daring the yard, crossing
to hope. My wife, compliant
to the call of lost
causes, insisted. And at long last,
a home. Something then
about his eyes, ancient, his careful
claws, like a priest, dispensing
death, the threat, the lizard head,
the fallen chick, the mouse. All
in service of the court, all a
dispensation for the world to come,
home of the pharaohs.
A long life, but I remember most
his lying, spread-eagled, on my
chest, the deepening stare. I saw
a scarab, the cartouche he once
enshrined, the festivals
of forever. And he, he must have
wondered about my courting
of pleasure, the superficials, when
all along he was wedded so deeply
to paradise, to the days, the years,
the great golden tombs, the heavenly
houses of the gods.

Laying on Hands, North Georgia

Pop and sizzle of spirit. Sweat-soaked revival
on crutches, spinning wheelchair epiphany.

Late night bone rattle, babbling tongues, the
buzz saw souls chirring like cicadas. Rapture,

the circuit rider's lightning sparking on flesh.
Electric tarantella. Sudden seizures shaking

the spirit. Sometimes a whole hallelujah, like
a headstand or tumble in the charged air

of existence. Down to the altar, a cleansing,
a new world. They come on command. And

all night the lights dim and flash, the saints
sway, until nothing's left but dawn, early

doves on the wing, and the slight sprig of
paradise still lingering in the air.

Prophets

Promises unfulfilled, the desert demanded
justice. Imagine how they came howling
like the wind in a sudden storm,
sweeping through the Sinai like dust devils
or the lightning bolts of perdition.
What ragged impetuosity. What madness
as they chastised tribes and kings.
How frightening the roar of righteousness.
How startling the pillars of fire
as the people cowered, shivering in the shadows.
What were kings to do? Who could
argue with the whirlwind? The Ark rumbled.
The desert flicked its furious tongue.
The sand swirled and gathered into judgment.
O men of God, swing your staffs and rage,
rage until the moon's a bloodshot eye.

Abraham and Isaac

— *For Kierkegaard*

A late-night call, the resounding
whisper. Preparations began

immediately. A staff, the blade,
determination. Heads full of

trust and confusion. How many fathers
on the road? How many sons? Directly

to Moriah. Lightning in the glare of
duty. Rain for the meek. A strange

wind where nothing stirred. An altar.
Agony of renunciation. And when

the boy looked up he saw the steel in
his father's eyes. A promise lost,

a storm. Everything fading to darkness.
But suddenly, they rose and rejoiced.

Bewildered. Confused. They ran, they
staggered, they walked in sunshine and

shadow, together, all the way home, all
the way back to their love.

Barking While Music Stirs Among the Grasses and Leaves

The world has turned its back on you,
like a stranger,

and even friends have faces of stone.
Someone has put

you out in the yard on a short leash
in the cold rain

of indifference. No matter. You always
have a night

of constant barking to look forward to.
The neighbors surely

won't mind and all that the plump moon
will do is just

hang there. Good time for the yelp of
indignation. The wind,

of course, will carry your complaints like
a letter of resignation

while, suddenly, music stirs among the grasses
and leaves, but you never

hear it, sweet and subtle, because you can't
become the bowl of

emptiness and silence and you miss everything,
everything pure and

peaceful in the song of the deepening dark.

One Thing at a Time

Just pour the tea,
just look into the eye of the flower.

— *Billy Collins*

So driven by the relentless road,
the bend in our days,
we lose the key and get
locked
in the trunk of memories,
or run ahead blindly
down the path of what's to come.
We know better.
Slow down, stay right here,
stop.
Arithmetic of existence.
The pinprick of self
as improbable as
the world itself.
Death is the only flower.
Look into its eye:

the old oak,
the lily,
the child.

Feel the trembling in us all.

Breaking Through to the Dolphins

Yes, they seem to be saying,
clicking and nodding
their heads.
Yes, we're here, waiting…
Tuning and re-tuning,
isn't it like your
grandparents' old radio,
the one with the broken dial,
the way you used to spin it
over and over,
crossing the fields of static
and sound,
until suddenly you found
at the far end of the line
a moment, a connection,
the most beautiful music
you'd ever heard?

Landscape of the Saxophone

Deep throated. Everything raw,
leaner. Mercies

in the reed. The blow's like a shiver,
fingers running

up and down a spine of notes.
Somewhere

in the stops something moving,
something risen.

A threnody. Pure notes like a
palimpsest.

Traces of truth. Spirit sounding
from below,

the rise and fall of breath. The voice
old,

fathomless, a deep bass rumbling,
pulsing in the trembling air.

To Nashville with George Jones

—*1970*

Fat tick of a Tennessee moon, bloodred.
Fast track to Music City,

pastures wide as your wide-eyed look
in the rearview mirror,

everything flying away like a memory.
The good times

are closer now, close as a dream drifting in air,
but also this threnody

that everything is not always all right, that
whiskey and pain

are the wages of love. Harder times, too,
but nothing, nothing's ever as hard

as it seems, even dying. A harvest moon, hopeful,
settles in the sky.

And this, too, you seem to sense after so many miles,
is just the way it should be.

The Man in the Car

The man in the car behind you is angry
and impatient. Leaning on his horn,

he weaves through traffic like a man on
the run, popping the clutch of his days.

Sliding on the shoulders of the night,
he surges, sticks

a fender in your back. He's headed now
to everywhere and nowhere, bearing down

like an eighteen-wheeler on its way to
another world. Nothing but nights and

white line fever. Nothing but the cadence
of the road. Up ahead, at

an intersection far away as the wind, a light
changes, all the lanes converge toward

forever. The man in the car behind you
rockets through the rain.

Everything he sees is shining, everything swirls.
He guns his motor, he's alive,

exhilarated. Down the road, as far as the eye
can see, stars are

crystalline, everything's clear, everything gleams
like the eye of a beast.

Baby Needs New Shoes

— *Ode to Las Vegas*

Click and scatter of dice on a velvet throw,
that sudden rush

as your brain teeters on the tip of stiletto heels.
A crackling current

shoots through the air. Champagne and caviar
linger on your lips.

Fruit tumbles in the one-armed bandits as you
pull the lever

on your own execution, lost for hours in the
labyrinth, pumping

dollars for dealers. The little ball dancing
in its slot is nothing

less than a date with destiny. That croupier in the
cummerbund calls you

like a dog to the hunt. Razzle, dazzle, catch those
kings.

You're the odds-on bettor, bellying up to the bet.
Hit it one more time,

double down on desire. Shake and rattle those bones
till the sun wakes up,

splashes clouds in its face, and pops its first sweet beer
all across the morning sky.

Lilacs

— Gettysburg, 1863

Imagine the bright magenta whorls,
so delicate,

swaying in the sun, as if the sky
had gathered

itself one last time against the storm.
How quiet the hand

of beauty, how brilliant its gentle
touch.

Nothing, not even the stars, could
burst so full

of light. — There, in the fields, the
lilacs bowed.

The death beetle clicked, again and again.

Gettysburg

—*1913, Fiftieth Reunion*

A year before the Great One,
the war to end all wars.

The thin lines of blue and gray
in a stillness where nothing

stirred but memory. Pickett's
men, the few, came slowly

through the wheat on canes,
crutches, wheelchairs. An old

rebel yell here and there. And
the Union boys, tattered and

limping, echoed a reply. But no
fusillade, no cannons. Only

wizened warriors in the warm
summer air. Only friends now

holding one another closely.
Never again, they vowed. Never.

As the locusts whirred and the pines
seemed to lean in silent prayer.

Clotilda

—Last known slave ship to reach US soil in 1860

Behold the old skin war.
Greed opened like a vein,
blood thrower,
teacher of rank,
democracy of deadened life.
Caste was venom,
numbing the heart,
a sure anesthetic of the senses.
Cotton was king,
fear came coiled, poised like an asp,
ancient hooded beast.

***

Stubbornness, only flesh could be
subdued.
Spirit unchained. Generations
enduring the whip.
Songs of the fields, songs of another
world.
Resistance, an inner fist.
Men and women of solemn gestures
bowed deeply,
spirit to spirit.
The snake began to die.

The Last Days of Buffalo Bill Cody

Even the horses knew
a shadow had come round,
the last proud laps,
the twilight of a man.
He rode the wind once,
quick as a line of lightning,
lean as a hawk on the wing.
Heart of the hunt,
pulse of the rumbling
earth.
But this is the moon
blurring to black,
cold as the gathering rain.
This is the night.
And there, in the dark,
at the edge of the timber,
far up, a eulogy —
a lone wolf calling till dawn.

Sitting Bull

Sometimes a bit of tobacco
and an old blanket,

dreaming under the stars.
What visions

the old chief had. Soldiers
raining from the sky,

victory camps, the hard trail
of defeat.

Daguerreotypes in London
where he kicked up

the dust again of a distant life.
Cigar-store Indian.

But even at the end, his own
men coming

to do the deed, blood was like
a blessing.

Trembling leaves — something
stirred, the blur

of a man. Nothing there, nothing
but the wind

moving in the trees, gone when
they turned and stared.

Villa

Don't let it end like this. Tell them
I said something.

— *Last words of Pancho Villa*

Perhaps the wind carried your words
to the last sentence
and beyond.
The sun witnessed your hands,
how they had a grammar,
a fury all their own.
Your eyes were a language of fire.
But no man outlives himself,
only the shadow
of what he could not be.
The sky darkened,
rifles took you away.
You thought of Mexico,
her glorious flowers.
You remembered how they fade,
how they always come again.

Postscript to Castro

You gave us hope, the one thing
that didn't crack

like leather in the sun. You were
a child promised

by the wind. We watered you even
as a seed

and dreamed of land no one owned.
Mucho gusto:

the reason, the relish of our labor.
The sky was open,

the flowers were tall and holy.

* * *

We pull like an old horse that takes
to the plow

in its dreams. We file once again
past Ché's hands

under glass, your uniform in the corner.
Relics of the Bay of Pigs.

Such is time's debris, the tired furniture
of our youth.

Now that god has not come, we ask only
for sugar,

a little coffee, a quiet stone by the sea.

Water

Here lies One
whose Name was writ in Water.

—*Keats's gravestone*

Rome and the old cemetery, Keats
long at rest.

Everything is water, Thales said.
The one and the many.

Endless waves rising and falling,
the sea of eternity.

The self, shape-shifting, aqueous,
never the same,

like language swimming in the
tides of time.

Or priests returning sand mandalas
to streams.

Keats's words, supple and strong, always
swirling,

circling in the currents, coming and going,
shining,

his pure poems pulsing again and again,
like the music of the stars,

the fountain of the spirit.

Prisoner

A prisoner of smells, I would rather eat than pray.
— *Theodore Roethke*

You will do no penance. No dried
bark of the anchorite.

No locusts. Only honey, delicacies
of the day.

The great gods of glaze, heavenly chocolate.
They beckon.

Come eat. Go down to dust with the lather
of cream on your tongue.

Hands awash in pudding. Sugar crumbs
leading you home.

You must listen and obey. Eternity can wait.
Sweet heaven is now, the sublime,

the promise of ecstasy. Glorious, these jewels,
these victuals of joy,

licking your lips, enchanted, even unto the end.

Krishna at the Potter's Wheel

We fools, we cut our poems out of air.
— *Gwendolyn Brooks*

You cut your poetry from clay. Spirit
to water and whirl,

shaping shapes that come and go.
Smoothing up

and down, round and round, like
lives lived

passing through. Turning and turning
we see your swirl,

a glint of forever flowering in the flow.
You knead your

share of comings and goings. Isn't it like
being in love

with the world? But love is surrender.
The hand that takes

finds nothing there; close your fist around
the air. Leaner and

leaner, nothing's lost is all the art —
cutting strings

the only way to catch the heart.

International Day of the Disappeared

Where are they? Colors of the moonless night.
Motes in the eye of the sun.

Cast the widest ears. Every note lost in the wind.
They cannot be found,

these shadows on the seas of departure, the dirt
roads of desperation.

Prisons, back alleys, miles of homeless tents.
Ghosts gone away,

leaving what once was there, memory treading
just above water

as the past falls to fog. Harder to see what isn't
there, harder to hope.

A Kaddish for the dead? No, not yet. Tomorrow's
like a loose thread,

hands round the skein of thin air.

Avant-garde

What dandies the dogwoods are! And how
these daisies

in their yellow coats are insouciant as young bloods
strutting down

the boulevard. Unmannerly, the dollar weeds are
elbowing in the grass.

Impatiens do a cartwheel of colors. And if the new
willows toss their hair

and run wildly in the wind this can only mean that
suddenly

spring has stepped into the field, cocked its old beret,
and left us once again

speechless in the sun.

Summer

Like some great mistress
of the sun,
once again
your casual blouse
is open in the fields,
roses blushing,
a choker of oleander
sparkling round your neck.
Wild jasmine in your hair.
Ambrosia of honeysuckle
and lilting magnolias.
Fire in the grass at your feet.
With the sudden burn of your being,
you take us quick and hard
in the heat.
Madness for a short season.
Then you cool and turn away,
leaving rust in the trees.
Soon
you send a letter in the leaves:
the first frost
is the cold kiss of goodbye.

The Body's Hope

The shoulders, at long last, wave
the tired hands of surrender.

Enough, they say. The back's
like an old bridge sagging in

the rain. It sways and creaks.
No mas, it says. *No mas.* Legs,

like fallen plinths, concur. Too
many miles on their feet. *Slow*

down, says the crooked neck. And
the head, wizened, bows down as if

praying for a pillow. A place it can
sleep. And dream. But not of collapse.

Or death. The body wants a world of
water. Buoyancy. Joy. It wants to swim.

Light-limbed, it wants to float forever,
like a wave. Or driftwood. It dreams of

radiance, faraway lands. Sailing, its only hope
is moonlight, wind, the soft hands of the sea.

What's Behind You

Think of the old fat man at the state fair
who runs the Black Hole Machine
so well that everything gets sucked into it.

All those moments that were issued to you
like tickets. Your big plans for the Ferris Wheel,
the freak shows, even the clown who gets dunked

in the tank, gone in a twinkle, as what will be
races like a madman on fire into what was.
Pictures? Fodder for the shoebox.

Mementos? Do you think that carnival doll
is worth a hundred dollars? Ever tried
to find any memories in the House of Mirrors?

Good luck. The fat man burps, cranks his machine
a little faster, and you can say goodbye to a fistful
of tickets, like water swirling down the drain.

But you knew all this at the door. You knew
the look in his eyes, the huge stomach,
the insatiable hunger. No matter.

Try to love the colors, the barking of the carnies,
the wild laughter of the moment as you plunge
headlong like a kid down the waterslide of the night.

Wild Words

Dictionaries are the graveyards of language.
— *Simon Dentith*

Not unlike that famous Remington,
the one of the weary bronc-

buster, wearier bronc. Both
worn in the saddle. Tired and

spent. Exhausted. And you said: *Let
them loose!* in your slew of sudden

words, free, frenetic, ranging
wild across my ears. Something

in the air. Brambles, tumbling
sagebrush. Dust devils. A

summer sandstorm of every
syllable. And I said: *Say

it again!* just as all the
Appaloosas reared and rushed

like desert jinn, surging and unstoppable,
in the charging ions of the air.

Alchemy

Today you'll gather the glow,
throw wide the windows

of your house. You'll scatter
the vowels,

sibilants formed and spit,
metaphors

sparkling like sunlight on glass.
You'll open

a tincture of verbs, bubble quicksilver
on the skin of things,

bead the dross of dust. You'll spark,
turn the words

to wine. You'll burn, catch the core,
the glint again of gold.

Writing

A good day. A few sentences.
One that almost has the feel of the true.

—*Flaubert*

Begin anywhere, but only
with ammonia, the crispest
clove, the kind of herb that
dizzies, even stuns, the most
jaded nose. If your head is not
snapped back in the sun,
start again.
Somewhere in the middle
you'll find a road not on any
map, a path that wasn't there
until you threw away the stars
and let the dreaming moon
take you by the hand.
Blindly, but not alone, go then
where you have to go.
Step lightly with the wind.
And if there is an end,
let it be like those deer staring
in the last light, their haunting
eyes, the way they linger,
the way they follow you
in the deepening dark of the night.

© Parker Stewart

John Valentine has a Ph.D. in philosophy from Vanderbilt University and taught at various colleges and universities for forty-six years, including the University of Alabama in Birmingham, East Georgia State College in Swainsboro, and the Savannah College of Art and Design (SCAD). He retired from SCAD in 2022.

He is the author of the book *Beginning Aesthetics: An Introduction to the Philosophy of Art* and numerous articles in philosophy journals.

His poetry has been published in the collection *The Heart of the Matter*, the chapbook *Close to the Fallen*, and in *The Sewanee Review*, *International Poetry Review*, *The Midwest Quarterly*, *Mudlark: An Electronic Journal of Poetry & Poetics*, *Southern Poetry Review*, *Snake Nation Review*, and others.

His poems attempt to capture moments of sudden illumination that reveal the interconnectivity of all beings. He has been influenced in this regard by Zen Buddhism and the literature of existentialism and also by William Blake's famous lines from "Auguries of Innocence":

> To see a World in a Grain of Sand
> And a Heaven in a Wild Flower
> Hold Infinity in the palm of your hand
> And Eternity in an hour...

Poetry is a dance between the universal and the singular, the one and the many. When we can suddenly intuit and grasp the dance, we come closer to empathy and appreciation for every life-form on our planet.

monte ceceri

In the early 1500s, it was from the heights of Monte Ceceri — otherwise known as "Swan Mountain" — in Fiesole, Italy, that inventor and artist Leonardo da Vinci let soar one of his experimental flying machines.

Envisioning a future where such fantastical creations would one day become reality, Leonardo desired to fill the world with awe-inspiring inventions and ideas.

Like its namesake's Renaissance roots, Monte Ceceri Publishers supports avant-garde writers whose works challenge current perspectives, inspire new paths, and speak to a modern-day humanism.

Based in Savannah, Georgia, Monte Ceceri is an independent publisher of books that raise issues of social, cultural, and philosophical interest, cross disciplinary boundaries, and facilitate cross-cultural dialogue through effective and engaging writing.

SwanHorse Press is an imprint of
Monte Ceceri Publishers, LLC

www.ingramcontent.com/pod-product-compliance
Lightning Source LLC
Chambersburg PA
CBHW060536080526
44586CB00012B/751